Sommario

INTRODUCION: ....

   5 tips for cooking with children.. 0

Chapter 1 12
   Rules for successful cooking 13
   Tips for new chefs 14
   Artisan Baker 21

Chapter 2 25
   Uses and benefits of almond flour 25

Cooking Base 31
   Required equipment 34
   Ingredients for cooking flour 35
   Sweetener 38
   Essential oil 41
   spices 43

Chapter 3 44
   Some of the most popular bread usually eaten at breakfast, lunch, or dinner are: 44

RECIPES: 47
   Instant bread 48
   Flaxseed bread 50
   Cloud bread 51
   Quick coconut bread 54
   Blackberry bread 56
   Coconut flour bread 58
   Chocolate bread and peanut butter 61
   Zucchini and nut bread 63
   Almond flour bread 64

- Cauliflower Bread 67
- Garlic bread and cheese 68
- Cheddar chives 70
- Pumpkin bread 71
- Sesame bread 73
- Farm yeast bread 75
- Banana Bread 77
- Cinnamon bun 79
- Gluten-free bread cheese 81
- Garlic, rosemary, and bread 83
- Garlic Cheese Bread Muffins 85
- Coconut Zucchini Muffins 87
- Cinnamon and Apple Spice Muffins 89
- Cranberry Orange Bread 91
- Lemon and Poppy Seed Roll 93
- Blueberry muffins 96

Chapter5 98
Low-carb chocolate candy 98
- Chocolate cup and toasted almonds 98
- Chocolate bomb 100
- Chocolate and coconut bombs 101
- Fried chocolate bomb chain 102
- Chocolate high heels with big sunflower seeds chocolate 103
- Coconut chocolate 104
- Keto Chocolate Cookies Keto Chocolate Ice Cream Shower 106
- Shower and chocolate ice cream 107
- Ketone and coconut chocolate 109
- Coconut ketose 110

Dark chocolate ketone pump	112
Lightweight chocolate and coconut high heels	113
Berry fat gun	115
Blueberry Ketone Butter Gun	116
Strawberry cream	117
Pudding lemon and blackberry	119
Lemon Cheese Pancakes Fried Lemon Coconut Mussels	120
Coconut and lemon bomb	122
Coconut cake, poppy seeds and lemon	123
Lemon Pump Ketone	125
Nut and berry pancakes	126
Raspberry and lemon ice pump	127
Strawberry Ketone Fat Pump	128
Carrot pancakes	129
Almond Cookies	132
Coconut fat pump Keto coconut oil pump	133
Coconut ketone oil pump	135
Cheese balls	136
Greer Ferrero-Rocher-Qin Kai	138
"Truffle" Ketone	138
Greer Ferrero-Rocher-Qin Kai	139
"Truffle" Ketone	140
Philadelphia Cream Cheese Ketone Pump	142
Bite from Ketone Brownie	144
Easter "pancakes"	145
Ketone Fund Award	146
Keto Raffaella 16 pieces per hour	147
Low-carb egg cheese cake	149

Naples grease gun 151
Keto nuts and peanut butter sweet fruit 153
Pumpkin Pump.. 154
Pumpkin Cheese Egg Mousse 156

© **Copyright 2020 by Emily Williams**
All rights reserved.

This document is geared towards providing exact and reliable information with regards to the topic and issue covered. The publication is sold with the idea that the publisher is not required to render accounting, officially permitted, or otherwise, qualified services. If advice is necessary, legal or professional, a practiced individual in the profession should be ordered.

- From a Declaration of Principles which was accepted and approved equally by a Committee of the American Bar Association and a Committee of Publishers and Associations.

In no way is it legal to reproduce, duplicate, or transmit any part of this document in either electronic means or in printed format. Recording of this publication is strictly prohibited and any storage of this document is not allowed unless with written permission from the publisher. All rights reserved.

The information provided herein is stated to be truthful and consistent, in that any liability, in terms of inattention or otherwise, by any usage or abuse of any policies, processes, or directions contained within is the solitary and utter responsibility of the recipient reader. Under no circumstances will any legal responsibility or blame be held against the publisher for any reparation, damages, or monetary loss due to the information herein, either directly or indirectly.

Respective authors own all copyrights not held by the publisher.

The information herein is offered for informational purposes solely, and is universal as so. The presentation of the information is without contract or any type of guarantee assurance.

The trademarks that are used are without any consent, and the publication of the trademark is without permission or backing by the trademark owner. All trademarks and brands within this book are for clarifying purposes only and are the owned by the owners themselves, not affiliated with this document

INTRODUCION:

One way to solve the most demanding taste buds in a family is to let children into the kitchen first.

5 tips for cooking with children

The formula of green milk pistachio is a high starting point for children to healthy cooking.

1. Reserve time. Teaching children to cook requires patience and time. Don't worry; cooking will be safer and more enjoyable.

- Spend some time with your family; find out when most family members can take part in this fun game!
- Give extra time to sort out untidy recipes.
- Cooking in large quantities to prepare meals can save more time in the long run.

2. Let children choose the recipe. Children are more eager to cook for themselves!

- First look at the food in the fridge and food storage room and then find easy to follow and child-friendly recipes based on the food you have.
- Let your child choose freely between two recipes so that he doesn't mind too many choices.

3. Configure the workspace. Because the workplace is child-friendly in advance, cooking pressure can be reduced. Keep potentially hazardous kitchen utensils away from the workplace. Make sure the child can focus on the task. Arranging the workplace before taking children to the kitchen can alleviate parental stress and anxiety and put more emphasis on integration.

- If the child cannot use hot tools or knives when he is young, parents can cut and cook some items so that the child is responsible for the assembly process
- Rice bowls, salads, and parfait are tasty snacks that allow children to organize fruit and vegetables according to their creativity and motor skills.

4. Children help to prepare food. Depending on the child's age, they can help in cleaning, peeling, sowing, juice, measuring, or cutting the product.

- Sauce recipes are a great way to learn how to work.
- If the child is too small to slice the product, find a recipe that you can mix by hand, e.g., a vegetarian burger.

5. Let children make mistakes. Give him control and let the children feel confident in the kitchen. The recipe steps may be outdated, or the measurement results may differ slightly, but they can become more independent and encourage further help in the kitchen.

- Parents, please try it with you! If the measurement is incorrect, you can easily track Washington

Developing cooking skills for beginners means giving children access to the kitchen as a child. When they grow up and understand the equipment, ingredients and technology, they will become more independent and confident, and will be able to develop a love of cooking for life.

It is worth compiling an age guide for all cooking habits from scratch. Encourage and remind the baker:

- Read the recipe from start to finish, then measure, mix and follow the instructions. If you don't know the glossary, ask for help before continuing.
- Wash hands before handling food. Pinch long hair while working to avoid tangling (and eating!).
- When moving the pan to or from the oven, always use the shelf and turn the oven off after use.

Of course, cooking skills that children can master will depend on their age, agility and concentration time. The younger the children, the more they need help along the way. However, even the smallest hands have many ways to help. Before starting, consider the complexity of the formula. As mentioned in my book, some recipes contain levels of difficulty. Each has 1-3 rolling surfaces (three highest levels). New chefs can start with simple recipes and then gradually improve.

When you're ready to have fun, here are some long instructions for your home baker.

Preschool kids (2-5 years old)

Most young children and preschoolers like to cook. They do it with enthusiasm, and they like to mix, knead, and mix the dough on a baking tray. Encourage them to use their senses: they smell of spices like cinnamon, touch the taste of flour, and even taste the ingredients before entering the bowl. Children of this age will need much help from you. Most people do not have sufficient skills to make precise measurements or cannot read (or range of attention) to follow the recipe from start to finish. But give them many opportunities to pour the ingredients into the bowl and mix. This simple activity will give you great fun.

Young chef (6-8 years old)

Elementary school students have mastered excellent motor skills and have a good understanding of essential reading and mathematics, so they can follow simple recipe instructions to measure ingredients. They can also perform tasks such as fat and casserole on exciting dishes, breaking eggs, screening, brewing, brewing, making and decorating decorations. Encourage the young chef to carefully follow the recipe steps while working, but hold them tight to make sure they are in the best condition, and if they are not suitable, you should intervene.

Before teens (9-12 years old)

Older children can perform more complex tasks, such as electric mixers or food processors and baking food. It is the perfect time

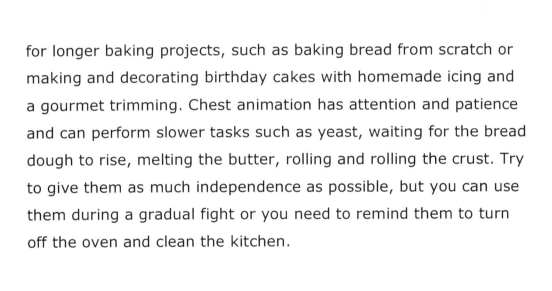

for longer baking projects, such as baking bread from scratch or making and decorating birthday cakes with homemade icing and a gourmet trimming. Chest animation has attention and patience and can perform slower tasks such as yeast, waiting for the bread dough to rise, melting the butter, rolling and rolling the crust. Try to give them as much independence as possible, but you can use them during a gradual fight or you need to remind them to turn off the oven and clean the kitchen.

Chapter 1

Cooking rules

Cooking rules are essential because they guarantee our safety during cooking. Even adults can cut their fingers or get burned. I need to practice! In this book, you'll find some rules for using knives and ovens, but they also include rules such as washing fruit and vegetables, creating jobs, and when to ask adults for help.

It's time to review all the specific cooking rules that are not listed here.

Here are six essential rules for every kitchen:

1) Always cook with adults. Some steps require adult help.

2) Hand washing. Our hands carry bacteria, so washing your hands is very important. Before cooking, wash your hands with warm soapy water and scrub for 20 seconds (singing "Twinkle, Twinkle and Little Star" twice).

3) Wash fruit and vegetables.

Bacteria and dirt are also found on fruit and vegetables. Rinse with running water before use and wipe gently. You can use a hand or soft brush.

4) Safe handling of eggs and meat.

Raw eggs and meat may contain harmful bacteria. Wash your hands after touching raw eggs. Use other knives and chopping boards for raw meat. Wash hands before and after touching raw meat.

5   Prepare the workspace.

The first step is to clean the counter in which you will "prepare" ingredients (prepare them). Wipe the worktop with a clean damp cloth or sponge. Then bring all the ingredients and tools that you will use in the workplace.

6) Easy cleaning

After all, you don't need too many dishes! When using spoons, pans, frying pans and other kitchen utensils, allow them to cool if necessary, and then put them in the dishwasher or wash and discard. It will save you later.

Rules for successful cooking

These rules may differ from yours at school. Although some rules are for security reasons, other rules are smarter than working harder. Even television cooking specialists will tell you that they have not read the recipe entirely and should stop all operations and run out of ingredients.

1) Live with an adult. For young people to cook, every family has different rules. Consult an adult before starting. Show them the recipes you are planning and decide together whether you need help, steps or instructional tools.

2) Read the recipe twice. Before you start, read the recipe you plan to make at least twice. Thorough knowledge of ingredients, tools and activities will ensure smoother cooking.

3) organization. It is easy to prepare for success in the kitchen; before you start cooking or cooking, be as organized as possible. It is essential to prepare the ingredients in advance and clean them thoroughly. The following two tips can provide each home chef with some best practices in these areas.

Tips for new chefs

Watch movies of famous chefs and their skills. Whether you are chopping onions perfectly or grilling meat, you can learn it!

   Prepare in advance.

Before purchasing formula ingredients, you should quickly make an inventory of food in the pantry, refrigerator, spice cabinet and / or in the garden. Then enter your needs. Then carefully check the following list: when cooking, you suddenly realize that some ingredient is missing, which is not interesting.

Prepare the land.

Imagine your favorite TV boss. What is your workspace You need to set your own rules, such as keeping the work surface clean and measuring the ingredients (see 8 tips for organized chefs)?

Do one job at a time.

Cooking requires concentration, especially while learning. Cooking many dishes at the same time is like juggling. You will master it; I just need some practice. Start slowly and gradually perform more complex tasks.

Store ingredients or tools after cleaning and use.

Clear spills immediately.

Wash agricultural products.

 Even if you plan to peel, always use clean hands or a clean vegetable brush to clean fruits and vegetables. When cutting agricultural products with a knife, the knife carries dirt and bacteria from the outside in. Dry the clean product with a clean cloth or paper towel. Remove and discard the outermost lettuce, cabbage and Brussels sprouts.

Remember to wash your hands.

Whenever you touch raw meat, sauce, raw eggs, fresh products or dirty dishes, you should start with clean hands and wash your hands with warm soapy water. Oh, sure, every time you try to make a product using Chinese recipes.

Electrical safety.

Keep kitchen utensils and small appliances away from water sources to reduce the risk of electric shock.

Use a knife carefully.

Take extra care when holding the knife, especially if you have a younger brother in your family. Do not turn your hand abruptly. When not in use, put it down and make sure it is out of the reach of small children.

Keep warm and safe.

Remember to wear kitchen gloves and mats. To remember that the pan is hot, put the oven gloves on or out of the oven and slide it on the handle. After using the oven or other kitchen utensils, turn them off.

Baking dishes

Your warehouse is a place where you wait for raw materials! The first general rule for delicious baking begins with high-quality ingredients. The right ingredients are important, but fresh ingredients are just as important as the highest quality ingredients. In some cases, if the right choice is not made, the ingredients can be replaced, but sometimes replacing the ingredients in the dough can be disappointing. It is a common ingredient used in many cake recipes.

yeast

The powder is a raising agent and can increase baking. Store in a dry, cool place. You can check the expiration date, but usually it should be replaced every six to twelve months. An interesting experiment is to check if the baking powder is bad: add 1 teaspoon of baking powder⅓ A cup of hot water. If there are too many bubbles in the mix, you can still use baking powder.

Sodium bicarbonate

Like baking soda, baking soda is a yeast used for baking. Baking soda and baking powder are different and cannot be replaced. Unlike baking powder, baking soda powder must add acid to the formula to work. You can check the expiration date, but baking soda should also be replaced every six to twelve months. An interesting way to check if baking soda is good: stir about 1 teaspoon baking soda Glass A glass of acidic things like lemon juice or vinegar. If there are too many bubbles in the mixture, you can always use baking soda.

butter

Butter is used in many cake recipes. There are two main types of butter, unsalted and salted. Most recipes require the use of unsalted butter, so you can control the amount of salt by adding salt alone. Check your recipe to see if the butter should be cold, softened or melted at room temperature. Even if you are in a hurry, do not exchange one person for another. Do not use margarine or oil instead of butter, unless the recipe says it's okay. Butter can be stored at room temperature for a short time, but should usually be stored in the refrigerator.

chocolate

There are many types of this popular cuisine: the most common are sugar free, dark, bitter and semi-sweet. Chocolates without sugar (which taste bad in themselves) are usually found in bars, and dark, sweet-bitter and semi-sweet chocolate can be used as flakes or bars. Some recipes require the use of unsweetened cocoa powder. It is a powder and does not contain sugar. Chocolate can last a long time, but for best results it should be stored in a cool, dry, dark place. It is not recommended to put chocolate in the fridge, because the cocoa butter will separate from the chocolate, which will make the chocolate "bloom" and form a gray film outside. It is safe to eat, but not very beautiful!

. Cream and milk

Sour cream made of butter is a delicacy for many baked goods. If you do not know this type of cream, the next time you visit the supermarket, pay attention to different types of cream. Heavy cream is the highest content of liquid cream and consists of at least 36% fat. Pure cream has a fat content of 30% to 36%. Thick light cream should be stored in the fridge. It can be used in most cases, but whipping heavy cream will provide a more stable and slightly denser cream.

The fat content of milk is also different. Whole milk has the highest fat content, followed by 2%, 1%, and then skimmed (without fat). When cooked with milk, skim milk produces more exceptional, more hydrated baked goods.

Before using, first, check the expiry date of the cream and milk in the container. The screening test will also show if the dairy product is fresh. Generally, cream and milk should be used within two weeks after opening.

Recipes are a method that will guide you in cooking dishes or meals.

Here are six tips on how to read recipes, prepare ingredients, and use them safely in the kitchen.

1)   Read the recipe. Each recipe has a title that tells you what it is. The recipe also gives the preparation time, serving size, list of ingredients, list of necessary tools, and cooking instructions. Before you start cooking, read the entire recipe to understand your expectations throughout the process.

2) Make sure you have all the ingredients. Read the list of ingredients and make sure they are already at home. Otherwise, make a shopping list and let adults enter the store.

3) Learn about all ingredients and tools. Before cooking, remove the necessary tools and ingredients that are very useful so that nothing can be found in the kitchen when cooking on the stove.

4) Measure carefully. This is important when cooking, but it is really important when cooking. Make sure all flavors and ingredients are at the measurement level. (You can ask an adult to tell you how to do this).

5 be careful. When using sharp tools (such as knives, peelers or graters), always grow with you. Before you begin, discuss with your adult assistant the available tools and ways to use them safely.

6) Make sure the stove and oven are safe. Practical safety is very important when using an oven or oven. the most important is:

Do not start cooking after growing up.

Do not touch the pan on the burner or stove, as they may be hot.

Never leave the oven unattended.

Never place an empty pan on a hot burner.

Always pinching long hair and roll up your sleeves.

It always grows when cooking.

Always wear kitchen gloves to remove anything from the oven or oven, or ask an adult for help.

Artisan Baker

Cooking with children is a social interaction experience because children can gain valuable life skills. As adults, we lead, support, and explain each step of the process so that children can acquire knowledge and experience in a specific order and take the next step in a specific order.

One way to help children complete this process is to visualize them. For example, we can print process photos and simple measurement and mixing instructions in A5 card format. The cards can be arranged in the correct order, starting with the ingredients on the first card, to the required dishes, bowls and measuring/spoons on the second card, and then gradually measuring, mixing and mixing. Create. It's an easy-to-understand way in which children can think about what will happen and what will happen.

During the cooking process, children gradually understand the following concepts:

Mathematical measurements teach them fractions. When you cut the dough, ask him to divide it.

Reading skills: Improve your understanding and vocabulary when your child follows the instructions.

Teamwork: Work together to build relationships to create delicious food.

Curiosity: baking stimulates scientific curiosity; for example, it encourages children to wonder why the dough is growing.

Please be patient, follow the recipe step by step, and wait for the result.

From buying raw materials to baking, cleaning and finally testing baking - project work will teach children the value of project implementation.

Life skills: Improve your knowledge of food hygiene and safety, food sources, healthy diet and label content.

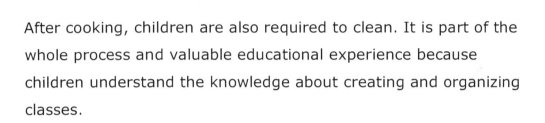

After cooking, children are also required to clean. It is part of the whole process and valuable educational experience because children understand the knowledge about creating and organizing classes.

Kitchen safety is crucial and requires constant monitoring. Make sure the area is clean, tidy and ready for cooking. Children should pay attention to the oven, oven components and other potential hazards.

Remember to allow everyone to wash their hands before promoting hygiene.

Chapter 2

How to eat more fat

The primary sources of fat in the keto diet are dairy products and high-fat eggs. There are many other sources of fat, including various vegetable oils, which can replace animal fats commonly used in cooking and baking. Some of these fat sources are:

coconut oil

MCT oil

Avocado oil

olive oil

Red palm oil

Drinks allowed in the ketone diet

Water is the most recommended drink for keto lovers. In addition to water, you can also drink coffee and tea, but do not add sweeteners, especially sugar. A small amount of milk or cream can be added to coffee or tea, but latte coffee is not allowed. Sometimes you can drink a glass of wine.

Uses and benefits of almond flour

When eating low-carb foods, ketone dieters or anyone in the kitchen can use many alternatives to wheat flour, but almond flour is considered the best choice in this aspect. Almond flour is not only low in carbohydrates but also relatively sweet. It is also rich in various nutrients, which can improve human health.

There are countless benefits of adding almond flour to the diet. The two most important aspects that should be mentioned here are lowered insulin resistance and lowered lousy LDL cholesterol.

This chapter tells you why almond flour is the best choice for eating low-carb foods.

Almond flour is obtained by grinding almonds. First, wash the almonds in boiling water to Eradicate the skin. In the second stage, the almonds are ground, and in the third and final stages, they are sieved and converted into ultra-healthy, delicious fine flour for the consumption of ketones or low-carb.

Someone confuses the names of almond flour and almond flour. Almond flour differs from almond flour in that almond flour does not bleach or Eradicate the skin during the manufacturing process. Grind the almonds to complete the peel, then turn it into almond flour.

Almond flour has high nutritional value in all respects because its ounce contains 14.2 grams of fat, 5.6 grams of carbohydrates, 6.1 grams of protein, and 163 calories.

Heart disease and cancer are currently one of the leading causes of death worldwide. Almond flour proved to be a very powerful weapon, not only to protect the body from heart disease and cancer, but also to prevent other diseases or health problems encountered by the body.

Free radicals are very dangerous molecules produced in the human body, they will destroy cells and accelerate the aging process. However, the vitamin E provided by almond flour acts as an antioxidant and prevents our body from producing this harmful molecule.

Another potent nutrient in almond flour is magnesium, which can lower blood pressure, insulin resistance, and blood sugar.

Foods made with traditional wheat flour are low in fat and high in carbohydrates, which eventually leads to fatigue and hunger. On the other hand, food cooked with almond flour is rich in healthy fats and low in carbohydrates, which has a positive effect on the overall health of the human body and has many advantages.

Because of all these characteristics, almond flour has a low glycemic index, so it can control the incorporation of sugar in the blood, thereby significantly helping diabetic patients maintain balance.

Magnesium is an essential mineral in almond flour and is responsible for controlling blood sugar. Studies have found that many people with type 2 diabetes lack magnesium in their blood. In this case, we can say with certainty that almond flour is the ideal choice to solve this problem.

Almond flour has a low and excellent glycemic index because people without type 2 diabetes can also benefit from almond flour if they face magnesium deficiency or want to control weight gain quickly.

Gluten is a protein found in traditional wheat flour, which is very harmful to people with celiac disease. What happened is that the body's immune system (called the autoimmune system) tried to eliminate this harmful protein, and as a result, the intestinal mucosa was damaged and problems such as rashes and diarrhea occurred. The benefit of almond flour is that it is gluten-free and wheat-free, so for those who need to eat less wheat-free and gluten-free foods in their diet, almond flour is an ideal choice for baking recipes.

Even if you know that almond flour is gluten-free, you should check the packaging when shopping because some brands add it to the product.

In today's world, many people die of heart disease every day. The two most important factors leading to heart disease are low cholesterol levels and high blood pressure. Multiple studies have shown that almonds are very effective in reducing harmful cholesterol levels in the body. If you have cholesterol problems and eat almonds regularly every day, you will find out in a few weeks.

Hypertension can also be treated by overcoming magnesium deficiency in the body. Almonds are a good source of magnesium. If you eat almonds regularly or add flour to your daily diet, it will be very different.

There is no doubt that when the wheat flour contained in the baking recipe is replaced by almond flour, its nutritional value will increase. It is not only effortless and easy to use but also makes food delicious and healthy.
When we make chicken nuggets, grilled chicken breasts or fish fillets, we usually dip the beaten eggs and cover them with bread crumbs. Here, we can use almond flour instead of breadcrumbs,

which can not only bring new flavor but also increase the nutritional value.

Sandwiches, muffins, bread or anything baked with almond flour is smoother and denser than regular wheat flour.

Almond flour does not contain phytic acid. Phytic acid is an anti-nutritional ingredient in wheat flour, but it actually prevents the absorption of nutrients in food. Phytic acid prevents the absorption of iron, calcium, zinc and magnesium.

One thing to note is the presence of phytic acid on the tonsil skin. Therefore, it is useless to remember not to whiten almonds before grinding. Phytic acid has a fixed purpose, but, phytic acid is present in almond flour.

Therefore, if you need low-carbohydrate flour, choose almond flour, because when preparing a ketone formula, this excellent choice will be your ideal substitute.

Cooking Base

Cooking tips

Almond flour is different from almond flour: they are all made from almonds, but not the same. Almond flour is made from peeled almonds. Almond flour is made from almonds and skin. The deliciousness of almond flour makes it interchangeable with flour, but not with almond flour.

Use low-carb flour: You can use low-carb flour such as almonds or coconut flour for baking, but you should follow the recipe for low-carb baking carbs. You cannot replace all-purpose flour with almond flour or coconut flour.

Choose ingredients wisely: for example, if your recipe requires flax powder, use golden flax powder. Experienced bakers recommend using golden flax powder because it is smaller than regular flax powder.

Use butter and cream cheese at room temperature: Use dairy products at room temperature to mix well. 40 minutes before cooking, Eradicate eggs, cream cheese and other refrigerated ingredients. Unless otherwise stated, use eggs and liquids at room temperature.

Use of dairy products: Avoid milk and cream because it contains very few carbohydrates. If the recipe requires more liquid, add water or use almonds or unsweetened coconut milk.

Use baking soda or baking soda: Low-carbon baking soda requires baking soda or baking soda that is lighter than regular cooking. Low-carb flours (such as coconut flour or almond flour) are thicker than regular flour. Therefore, you need more propellant than the conventional formula.

Pour oil into the pan: low-carb noodles are more sticky than traditional recipes. Lubricate your baking mold well. You may need to spread butter on the butter before using parchment paper.

Choose only low-carb and low-carb recipes-do not try to convert regular recipes to a small number of carbohydrates because they will be ineffective.

If you have the experience, try: If you cook low-carb products multiple times, try to make your recipes.

Use softened butter and cream cheese. If your baking ingredients are too cold, they will not spread evenly and cause uneven cooking.

Do not pack unless otherwise stated: when measuring low-carb flour, do not pack unless otherwise stated.

Use unsalted butter: Unless otherwise stated, use unsalted butter.

Use large eggs.

The oven and cooker have different temperatures-so, please check the baked goods before the time runs out.

Melted chocolate: Use a water bath to melt chocolate, because the chocolate will slowly melt under mild heat.

Let it cool properly, and then the thinly sliced low-carb products continue to harden as they cool. Therefore, cool the pastry and then cut it into thin slices.

Required equipment

Ordinary electric mixer-this is an essential tool that allows you to use different speeds according to your needs.

Food processors can be used for many items.

Manual blender: Use this blender to mix, make a puree, emulsify, or stir eggs.

Silicone pad: makes cleaning easier

Mixing dish: measuring cup and
spoon used for cooking.

whip

Welding wire cooling net

Cooking board

Square shell

Muffin tin

Saucepan

Baking tray

Cake mold

mold

Ingredients for cooking flour

Almond powder

Compared to using wheat recipes, baking with almond flour is a quick and easy process.

Be careful not to confuse almond flour with almond flour. The latter includes whole almonds, plus skin and grated. In the former, the skin is Eradicated and therefore discolored. This is the main difference between the two.

It's easy to roast with almond flour. Trying to Burn will not disappoint you.

Almond flour is available in health food stores and many supermarkets. It is also widely used on the Internet.

Benefits of almond flour

A good source of vitamin E. If you want healthy skin and hair, this vitamin is very important. It has antioxidant properties and can protect your body from free radical damage.

Good source of copper. Copper in almonds can promote bone health.

Good source of protein. Almond flour is an excellent source of protein. A single cup of almond flour contains 25 grams of protein.

Eating almonds can promote brain health. Many nutrients in almonds are good for the brain. Tryptophan is just one of the nutrients beneficial to the brain in almonds.

Control bad cholesterol. Almonds lower LDL cholesterol in the body, which is the wrong type. Almonds increase LDL cholesterol in the body, which is the wrong type.

Promotes heart health. The nutrients in almonds are good for the heart and can help prevent heart disease. Magnesium in almonds can reduce the risk of heart attack, and folic acid can help prevent arterial blockages.

This can lower blood pressure. Potassium in almonds can help control high blood pressure.

lose weight. The fat contained in almonds is good fat, which can regulate appetite and prevent you from eating too much on the table.

Compared with flour-containing foods, eating foods containing almond flour can actually help you lose weight.

Protect diabetes. Almonds help regulate insulin levels in the blood and can prevent diabetes.

Prevent congenital disabilities. Folic acid in almonds can prevent congenital disabilities.

Rich in fiber. The high fiber content in almonds prevents constipation and helps food pass through the digestive system.

Apply to skin, nails and hair. Almonds contain B vitamins, which can promote skin, hair and nail health.

coconut powder

Coconut flour is finely ground, high-fiber dry coconut that remains after coconut oil is extracted. As a purely natural product with one ingredient, it is a healthy alternative to wheat and other gluten-free flours, and is suitable for various formulations that require flour. It also contains more protein than most gluten-free flours (including oat bran and flaxseed flour). The protein content is similar to buckwheat and whole wheat flour, so it is rich in nutrients and wheat.

Benefits of coconut flour

Maintain a healthy weight: Coconut flour is rich in indigestible fiber and feels full, without the extra calories from digestible carbohydrates. For example, a bag of bagels of coconut flour can better meet your needs than the exquisite products you buy. All of these helps maintain site control and a healthy weight. In addition, coconut flour itself is slightly sweet, so you can usually reduce the number of sweeteners used in recipes made with it, which means fewer calories and does not affect taste.

Cereals and gluten-free: Coconut flour is naturally gluten-free and is not a common food allergen (although the name coconut is actually a fruit, not a nut), so coconut flour is ideal for gluten-free and allergy-free ways . In terms of potential allergies or intolerance, many gluten-free cereals and grains (such as wheat and corn) are much higher.

Ideal for blood sugar: Blood sugar (also called blood sugar) is the amount of glucose that our blood depends on. After eating, blood sugar increases and our body responds to this increase by releasing a hormone called insulin to control blood sugar levels, so it will not increase much. On the other hand, the rapid decline in blood sugar is controlled by a hormone called glucagon, which stimulates the release of more sugar into our blood. Blood sugar balance has been working, especially after eating.

Sweetener

Some popular sweeteners are used to produce sativoside, mannose, xylitol and erythritol ketone bread.

Stevia Stevia is an aromatic herb produced in South America, especially in Brazil and Paraguay. Since ancient times, it has been used as a sweetener and medicine in these countries.

Stevia is a natural sweetener obtained from the leaves of the Stevia plant. It does not contain calories and carbohydrates, and its glycemic index is zero. Therefore, it is often used to reduce or replace sugar in recipes. In other words, its sweetness is ten to fifteen times that of other natural sweeteners, so it does not require too much stevia to sweeten the formula. Depending on the method of use, the taste may be somewhat bitter and will not be caramelized like other sweeteners. Therefore, it works best in small amounts and in recipes containing other sources of sweets, such as: B. Husband Maple Syrup or Fruit. .

Xylitol Xylitol is a refined form and is a white crystalline substance similar to edible sugar.

Los)-This is a low-calorie sugar, but as sweet and clean as expected. Due to the small number of sugar substitutes, there are many human factors. Allulose was first found in wheat and then in certain fruits, including raisins, figs and jackfruit. A small amount of Allulose can be used in candy, such as brown sugar, maple syrup and caramel sauce. Allulose is a simple sugar (monosaccharide) that can be automatically absorbed by the body without any calories. It is ideal for people who want to limit calorie intake. People drink low-content beverages and foods that contain low-calorie sweeteners (eg, allose).

Erythritol-It occurs naturally in certain fruits and mushrooms. It is produced industrially by enzymatically hydrolyzing corn starch to produce glucose, which is then fermented with mushrooms to produce erythritol. It has been used in Japan since the 1990s. It comes in the form of crystals and powders, the latter usually being the first choice. The taste is excellent, with little aftertaste and umami. Each gram contains 0.2 calories, which is equivalent to 5% sugar calories, and the sweetness is 65%. He is weak

GI (1) and calories are very suitable for diabetics and dieters. Unlike other sugar alcohols, gas and irritable bowel syndrome are less likely.

Nuts and seeds:

almond

Nuts

walnut

Brazil nuts

hazelnut

Macadamia

Cashew nuts

pumpkin seeds

Sunflower seeds

Chia seeds

sesame

Nut and seed butter (simple, no seasoning or sugar added)

Essential oil

olive oil

Avocado oil

flaxseed oil

MCT oil

coconut oil

Walnut oil

spices

All fresh and dried herbs are completely allowed.

Season the food with dry spices. Pay attention to mixed spices and mixtures, because they usually contain sugar.

Cinnamon: Use cinnamon as part of your daily plan to improve the activity of insulin receptors. Just add half a teaspoon of cinnamon to smoothies, smoothies or other desserts.

Nutmeg: The flavor of nutmeg is slightly nutty and adds warmth to your food. It is commonly used in desserts and curries. Nutmeg seeds are compounds that act as antioxidants in your body. It also has anti-inflammatory properties and can help alleviate poor health conditions such as arthritis, diabetes and heart disease. Basil: (1 whole leaf-0.5g net carbohydrate) You can use fresh or dried basil for best results. Its dark green color indicates that it also contains an excellent source of magnesium, calcium and vitamin K, which is very useful for bones. It also helps allergies, arthritis or inflammatory bowel disease.

Oat fiber is important because it has an excellent bread structure. Oat fiber is made by grinding oat shells, which are pure, insoluble fibers. As a result, the fibers in the digestive tract are neither decomposed nor soluble in water. Several recipes combine this friendly ketone ingredient and low carb ingredients. Note: Oat fiber is different from oatmeal made by grinding oats.

Clove: Clove has a spicy but sweet taste, but also contains powerful natural medicines, which contain effective preservatives and fungicides, which can help prevent arthritis, gums and toothaches, infections and reduce digestive diseases.

Chapter 3

Some of the most popular bread usually eaten at breakfast, lunch, or dinner are:

bread.

These are round or elongated pasta, and they are rectangular. Bread is provided in the form of white bread, multigrain bread, whole wheat bread, sago bread, and many other pieces of bread. Bread is the most common type of bread.

Bagel.

A muffin is a kind of bread that looks like a donut. Unlike ordinary bread, muffins are made by boiling in water before baking.

Pizza.

Pizza is bread with tomato sauce, cheese, meat, and vegetables. Pizza is made in Italy. Pizza can also be prepared with a loaf of bread.

Muffin.

Cakes are made and baked just like cakes, but cakes are a type of bread, not cakes. Cakes are usually eaten at breakfast and can be sweet or salty.

Breadstick.

Breadsticks are dry bread that looks like pencils and is often used as a measuring tool. Breadsticks originally came from Turin, Italy, and are often used as screwdrivers.

Cookies.

Biscuits are a type of bread made with wheat flour and water and come in many forms, such as rye and cereals.

RECIPES:

Instant bread

Ingredients:

1/2 teaspoon baking powder, double effect

1 tablespoon butter

- 1 egg

- 3 tablespoons flour

address:

1. When preparing the mixture, Warm up the oven or cooker at 380 ° F
2. Take the butter, melt it over medium temperature, and place it in a microwave-safe container.
3. Put baking powder, almond flour, and eggs into the melted butter in a container.
4. Blend all the ingredients until they are even.
5. Place in the microwave and stir for a minute and a half or until set.
6. Take a knife, move it around its edge, then twist to transfer it to the board.

7. Cut the steak in half, put it in the toaster, and then put it in the pan.
8. Place in the oven and cook for 16 minutes or until fully cooked.
9. Eradicate from the oven after cooking and enjoy it.

Flaxseed bread

Ingredients:

- 2 eggs
-
- flour
-
- baking soda
-
- 5 tablespoons olive oil
-

  salt

  4 cups coconut flour

  water

address:

1. When preparing the dough, Warm up the oven or cooker at 408 º F
2. Break the eggs into a container, add the egg whites, and blend with an electric mixer.
3. Add coconut flour, flax flour, baking powder, olive oil, water and sea salt.
4. Continue stirring until the batter is made. Make sure the dough is smooth.

5. Let the dough sit for a few minutes because flax and coconut flour must absorb moisture.
6. Line the baking sheet with parchment paper
7. place the dough on top.
8. Heat it in the oven for 45 minutes, or until a knife is inserted for cleaning.
9. When finished, eradicate it from the oven and enjoy delicious keto flax bread.

Cloud bread

Ingredients:

Tartar

salt

- 1/5 cup cream cheese
-
- 3 large eggs
-
- Garlic powder

address:

10. Take the eggs, break them up, then put their whites in a dish and mix them with an electric mixer.

11. Continue playing for at least one minute.
12. Pour the tartar cream on the beaten egg whites and beat for another minute until a soft peak appears in the mixture.
13. Take another dish and add cream cheese, egg yolk and garlic powder.
14. Mix all the ingredients until they are even.
15. Transfer the egg yolk mix into the protein mixture
16. Then mix with a spatula.
17. Line the baking sheet with parchment paper.
18. Transfer the mixture to a baking sheet and spread it evenly with a spoon.
19. Temperature of the oven should be 400 ° F,
20. Then place the pan in the oven for 30 minutes,
21. It will turn golden brown.
22. Once cooked, eradicate it from the oven and enjoy delicious dark bread.

Quick coconut bread

Ingredients:

- 1 egg
-
- Garlic powder
-
- 4 cups grated cheese
-
- 1/5 cup cooked spinach, drained

   Cream cheese

   Tablespoon almond flour

  Salt seasoning

address:

1. Heat the oven or cookware to 380 ° F, then wrap in parchment paper to prepare the baking sheet.
2. Place cream cheese and mozzarella cheese in a microwave-safe dish. Microwave for half a minute.
3. Make sure to keep stirring every 16 seconds to achieve a good mixing effect.

4. Add spinach, eggs and almond flour to the cheese mixture. Mix until uniform.
5. Transfer the mixture to the baking tray and smooth it. Sprinkle with salt and garlic powder.
6. Burn the oven for 16 minutes.
7. Cook for another 5 minutes or until the other side becomes crispy.
8. Eradicate from the oven immediately after cooking and enjoy.

Blackberry bread

Ingredients:

bread

- 4 cups fresh blueberries
-
- 2 tablespoons heavy cream
-
- Melted butter
-
- vanilla
-
- 6 eggs
-
- baking powder

2 tablespoons yogurt

16 tablespoons coconut flour

cinnamon

Granulated beverage

½ teaspoon

frosting:

- Heavy cream
-
- Vinegar powder
-
- 1/5 teaspoon grated lemon zest
-

Melted butter

A little vanilla

address:

1. Heat the oven or cookware to 380 ° F, then wrap the bread tray with parchment paper.
2. Add heavy cream, eggs, sour cream, vanilla, vinegar, cinnamon, baking powder, and salt.
3. Mix until all ingredients are thoroughly mixed.
4. Pour the melted butter into the mixture
5. Then we need to mix well.
6. Add coconut flour to the mixture and continue to mix until a smooth dough is formed.
7. Put a layer of dough on the bread tray, sprinkle blueberries on top, and continue to layer until the dough is used up.
8. Burn the knife in the heated oven for 60 minutes, or insert the knife into the bread until the knife is clean.
9. When finished, eradicate from the oven and set aside.
10. Put heavy cream, milk, lemon zest, melted butter, and a little vanilla in a dish and mix well.
11. Spread the prepared mixture on the bread and enjoy.

Coconut flour bread

Ingredients:

- 2 cups flour
-
- olive oil
-
- flax seeds
-
- 7 eggs
-
- 1 tablespoon soda
-

  coconut milk

   Teaspoon Xanthan Gum

   Tablespoon

  ground cinnamon

  salt

address:

1. Heat cookware to 380 ° F, then cook with 8x4 bread pan lined with parchment paper.

2. Put coconut milk, eggs and olive oil in a blender and mix all ingredients until all ingredients are well mixed.

3. Put coconut flour, flax seed powder, baking powder, xanthan gum and cinnamon powder in a blender
4. Blend thoroughly until all elements are fully mixed.
5. Add tower and salt to mix.
6. Blend until a plane dough is formed.
7. Place the dough in the bread tray.
8. Burn the pan in the oven for 50 minutes, or clean it with a toothpick inserted in the middle.
9. After cooking, eliminate it from the oven.
10. Let it cool for a while.
11. Place it on a shelf and allow it to cool completely. Cut into thin slices and eat delicious coconut flour bread.

Chocolate bread and peanut butter

Prepare information:

Ingredients:

- eggs
- 3 teaspoons baking soda
- 1/2 teaspoon stevia liquid vanilla
- 3 teaspoons liquid chocolate stevia
- 4 cups almond flour
- almond milk

peanut butter

2 ounces unsweetened chocolate

Vanilla extract

Salt

butter

address:

1. Heat the oven or cookware to 380 ° F, then wrap the bread tray with parchment paper.

Sprinkle 2 tablespoons of butter, then mix the remaining 3 tablespoons of butter with peanut butter and melt over medium heat.

3. Add almond milk, baking powder, liquid vanilla stevia, liquid chocolate stevia, almond flour and sugar-free chocolate. Mix all ingredients.
4. Add eggs, vanilla extract and salt to the blend and keep mixing until a smooth dough is formed.
5. Place the bread in the bread tray.
6. Melt a tablespoon of butter and chocolate, then pour stevia into the dough.
7. Burn in the oven for 50 minutes.
8. After cooking, take it away from the oven, let it cool for a few minutes, and then slice it into thin slices.

Zucchini and nut bread

Ingredients:
- Almond powder
-
- 3 teaspoons baking powder
-
- olive oil
-
- 3 eggs
-
- ¼ teaspoon ground ginger
-
- ½ teaspoon vanilla extract
-
- Teaspoon nutmeg

Erythritol

Chopped nuts

cinnamon

2 cups zucchini grated

salt

address:

1. Heat the oven or cookware to 380 ° F, then add grease to prepare the 9x5 baking tray.
2. Take a dish and add baking soda, almond flour, nutmeg, ginger, cinnamon, erythritol, and salt.
3. Mix all the ingredients until they fuse.
4. Use paper towels to Eradicate excess water from the zucchini.
5. Break the eggs in another dish, add the zucchini and mix well until everything is mixed together.
6. Slowly add the almond flour mixture to the egg mixture and continue to use a hand blender for mixing
7. Until a plane dough is formed.
8. Transfer the bread to the bread tray, sprinkle with chopped nuts,
9. Then press it up with a spatula.
10. Burn in a preheated oven for 65 minutes, or until the nuts begin to brown.
11. After cooking, eradicate from the oven and serve.

Almond flour bread
Prepare information:

Ingredients:

- 4 eggs
-
- Almond powder
-
- Warm water
-
- 3 teaspoons baking soda

Melted coconut oil

Plantain shell

salt

address:

1. When preparing the dough, warm the oven to 400 ° F
2. Place it in a bread jar filled with parchment paper.
3. Take a mixing dish, add almond flour, baking powder, psyllium husk, and salt.
4. Mix thoroughly till uniform.
5. Add coconut oil, eggs and warm water to the mixture
6. Continue to mix till a smooth dough is shaped.
7. Transfer the dough to the bread box.

8. Burn in the oven for half an hour, or until golden in appearance.
9. After cooking, eradicate it from the oven and enjoy delicious almond flour bread.

Cauliflower Bread

Ingredients:
- 6 egg
-
- 2 cups cauliflower rice
-
- Almond flour cup
-
- baking soda

  salt

- sunflower seeds
-
- sesame

  pumpkin seeds

address:

1. Heat the oven or cookware to 380 ° F, then use a box of parchment paper to make bread.

2 Take a dish and add almond flour, baking powder, psyllium husk, and salt.

3. Add cauliflower and eggs to the combination

4. Continue stirring until a smooth paste form.
5. Put the dough in the bread box and put it in with a spatula.
6. Sprinkle with sunflower seeds, sesame, and pumpkin seeds.
7. Place it in the warmed oven for 50 minutes or till its top turns brown.
8. After cooking, eradicate it from the oven, cold and cut into thin slices.
9. You can then eat amazing cauliflower bread.

Garlic bread and cheese

Ingredients:
- 1 egg
-
- 1 tablespoon chopped garlic
-
- Grated cheese
-
- 1 tablespoon fresh parsley
-

  almond flour

  baking soda

  1 Full fat cheese

  Season with a little salt

address:

1. In a microwave-safe dish, add chopped garlic, grated mozzarella cheese, fresh parsley, almond flour, baking powder, cream cheese, and salt.
2. Stir gently to mix the ingredients and microwave at high temperature for 70 seconds.
3. Take out at high power, put in the microwave, and stir for half a minute.
4. Break the eggs and continue to whisk until a smooth batter is made.
5. Transfer the dough to the baking sheet and give it some form of garlic bread.
6. Sprinkle some cheese on top if needed.
7. Burn at 425 ° F for 16 minutes,
8. till turn it into golden brown.
9. After baking, eradicate it from the oven and enjoy delicious bread.

Cheddar chives

Ingredients:

- Cheddar cheese
-
- boiling water
-
- coconut flour
-
- 1 tablespoon apple cider vinegar
-
- eggs
-
- parmesan

butter

2 tablespoons chopped chives

Psyllium husk powder

1 tablespoon baking soda

salt

address:

1. Heat the oven or cookware to 380 ° F, then wrap it with parchment paper to prepare the baking tray.

2 Take a mixing dish, add plantain turf, coconut flour, baking powder, and salt.

Mix all ingredients.

3. Add eggs and butter to the mixture and continue stirring until bread crumbs form.
4. Add apple cider vinegar and water to the mixture while stirring.
5. Add chives, parmesan, and cheddar to the mixture.
6. Continue stirring until a good paste is formed.
7. Place the baking tray in the oven and burn for 40 minutes or until golden brown.
8. Eradicate from the oven after cooking and enjoy it.

Pumpkin bread

Ingredients:

- 4 eggs
- Pumpkin Pie Spice
- 3 cups almond flour
- 4 cups pumpkin puree
- 2 cups coconut flour

3 cups butter

Erythritol

gluten-free baking powder

pumpkin seeds

sea salt

address:

1. Heat the oven or cookware to 380 ° F and prepare a 9x5 bread tray lined with parchment paper.

2 Take a large mixing dish, add pumpkin pie spices, almond flour, baking powder, erythritol, coconut flour, and sea salt. Mix all ingredients until uniform.

Sesame bread

Ingredients:

- 8 eggs
- ½ cup flax seeds
- 6 Ounce cream cheese
- sesame
- 2 cups melted butter
- Rice husk powder
- ¾ cup heavy cream

2 cups almond flour

Teaspoon fennel seed powder

4 cups coconut flour

3 teaspoons baking soda

salt

address:

1. Heat the oven or cookware at a temperature of 380 ° F, and then line the lining into a 4x7 shape.

2. In a mixing dish, add flax seeds, sesame seeds, plantain turf powder, almond powder, fennel seed powder, coconut powder, baking powder and salt.

3. Mix all ingredients.

4. Take another dish, add eggs, cream cheese, melted butter and heavy cream,

5. Take the dry mixture, add it to the wet mixture, and keep mixing until a smooth paste form.

6. Transfer the dough to the mold and make it from above with a spatula.

7. Burn in the preheated oven for 50 minutes or until it is inserted into the bread until the toothpicks become clean.

8. Immediately after cooking, eradicate it from the oven, allow it to cool on the wire rack and cover with the desired lid.

Farm yeast bread

Ingredients:

- 2 cups of wheat gluten
-
- 8 tablespoons olive oil
-
- 1/5 cup warm water, separate
-
- 2 teaspoons baking soda
-
- 1 bag of active dry yeast
-
- 1/2 cup flax seed powder

sugar

1/2 tablespoon melted butter

2 cups almond flour

salt

address:

1. Take a large dish, add half a glass of water, dissolve sugar, add yeast, cover with a towel for 7-16 minutes,
2. Until the mixture is foamy.

2. Take another large dish and add the vital wheat gluten, baking soda, active dry yeast, flax flour, almond flour, and salt.
3. Mix all ingredients until combined and sieved.

3. Add olive oil and 1 3/4 of water to the yeast mixture and mix well.
4. Mix the dry ingredients with the wet ingredients and continue stirring with a wooden spatula until thoroughly mixed.
5. Knead the dough for 2-3 minutes to prepare the dough.
6. Take a large glass dish, add butter and butter, then pour the dough into a ball.
7. Cover the dish with a towel and store it in an oven preheated to 165 degrees for 1 hour.
8. Brush the top of the dough with melted butter and Burn in a preheated 400 ° F oven for 50 minutes.
9. After cooking, eradicate it from the oven and let it cool for a few minutes,
10. Leave the dish and let the bread cool completely, ready to slice and enjoy.

Banana Bread

Ingredients:
- 6 large eggs
- 2 cups chopped nuts
- 7 tablespoons butter
- 3 cups almond flour
- 1/5 cup unsweetened almond milk
- 3 teaspoons gluten-free baking powder

sea salt

1/5 cup coconut flour

1/2 cup erythritol

3 teaspoons banana extract

3 teaspoons cinnamon

address:

1. Heat the oven or cookware to 380 ° F and prepare a 9x5 bread tray lined with parchment paper.

2 Take a large dish and add baking soda, almond powder, cinnamon powder, coconut powder and salt.

Mix all the ingredients until they fuse.

3. Take another large dish and mix erythritol and butter with a hand mixer.
4. Add almond milk, banana extract, and eggs to the butter mixture and mix well.
5. Add the dry ingredient mixture to the wet ingredient mixture and keep mixing until a smooth paste is formed.
6. Add chopped nuts.
7. Place the dough in the bread tray and smooth it from above with a spatula.
8. Burn for 65 minutes in a preheated oven
9. Until it is inserted into the bread until the toothpick becomes clean.
10. After cooking, Eradicate it from the oven
11. Before enjoying the delicious keto banana bread, let it cool.

Cinnamon bun

Ingredients:

- 2 tablespoons soft butter
-
- Almond powder
-
- 4 egg
-
- 5 1/5 cup erythritol
-
- 6 3 ounces cream cheese, softened
-
- 7 1 teaspoon vanilla

cinnamon

Cake cream

2 tablespoons

melted butter

1 teaspoon baking soda

address:

1. Heat the oven or cookware to 380 ° F, then spread the parchment paper on a 9x5 bread tray.
2. Break the eggs and place the yolks and white eggs in two dishes.
3. Use an electric mixer to mix cake cream with protein. Continue mixing until a smooth tip appears.
4. Add cream cheese, vanilla, butter and stevia to the egg yolk
5. Mix thoroughly.
6. Add almond flour, baking powder, and half a teaspoon of cinnamon powder to the mixture and mix well.
7. Take a small dish and add the rest of the cinnamon, erythritol, and melted butter.
8. Mix thoroughly.
9. Add the egg white mixture to the egg yolk mixture and mix with a spatula.
10. Place half of the mixture in a bread tray, pour butter and cinnamon powder on top, and add the remaining mixture.
11. Vortex with a straight knife.
12. Burn it in the oven for 50 minutes, or until it turns golden brown.
13. Take it out of the oven after cooking and enjoy delicious cinnamon bread.

Gluten-free bread cheese

Ingredients:
- 1/5 cup coconut flour
- 1/2 cup parmesan
- 5 ounces cream cheese, softened
- 1/2 teaspoon sea salt
- 1/5 cup butter, softened
- 2/4 cup almond flour

3 large eggs

3 tablespoons unflavored whey protein

1/2 cup grated cheese

A teaspoon of baking soda

A tablespoon of water

address:

1. Heat the oven or cookware to 380 ° F and prepare an 8x4 bread pan lined with parchment paper.

Put 2 butter and cream cheese in the food processor and mix.

3. Add coconut flour, parmesan, almond flour, eggs, whey protein, mozzarella cheese powder, baking soda, water, and salt.
4. Mix until the mixture is thoroughly mixed.
5. Place the dough in the bread tray.
6. Burn it in the oven for 40 minutes or until it turns light brown.
7. Eradicate from the oven when cooking.
8. Go to the rack to cool.
9. Eradicate from the pan
10. Let the bread cool completely.
11. Cut into slices and enjoy.

Garlic, rosemary, and bread

Prepare information:

Ingredients:

- ¾ cup almond flour
-
- 1½ cup grated cheese
-
- 2 tablespoons cream cheese
-
- ½ teaspoon garlic powder
-
- ½ teaspoon salt
- 1 egg
-
- 1 teaspoon vinegar

Garlic and rosemary butter

3 cloves garlic minced

2 ounces of butter (RT)

½ teaspoon fresh rosemary, chopped

½ teaspoon of sea salt

address:

1. Heat the oven or cookware to 380 ° F, then cook cream cheese and mozzarella cheese in a dish for 40 to 50 seconds, stirring further.
2. Add almond flour, garlic powder, garlic and rosemary butter, eggs, vinegar and salt.
3. Mix all the ingredients until they are thoroughly mixed and form a smooth paste.
4. Place the parchment paper on an 8-inch round shell and transfer the dough to the top.
5. Take a fork and use it to make small holes in the dough.
6. Place in a preheated oven and Burn for 16 minutes or until golden brown.
7. Eradicate from the oven and set aside to cool.
8. Put chopped clove garlic, butter, chopped rosemary, and sea salt into a dish
9. Mix thoroughly.
10. Spread the mixture on the bread, place it in a baking tray, and put it back in the oven for 16 minutes.
11. After cooking, eradicate it from the oven, ready to slice and enjoy.

Garlic Cheese Bread Muffins

Ingredients:

- 3 cups almond flour
- 1/2 cup sour cream
- 1/5 cup chopped cilantro
- 6 tablespoons melted butter
- 4 ounces grated mozzarella cheese
- 4 large eggs

2 cups cheddar cheese

5 cloves garlic, chopped and thinly sliced

3 teaspoons baking soda

Scattered sea salt

address:

1. Heat the oven or cookware to 380 ° F and fill the muffin tin to prepare the muffin tin.
2 3 Cut the garlic cloves and melted butter into small dishes and mix well.
3. Place the eggs, remaining garlic cloves, sour cream and salt in the food processor.
4. Mix until all ingredients are mixed.
5. Add parsley, baking powder, almond flour and cheese to the food processor mixture
6. Continue processing until the dough becomes smooth.
7. Pour half of the dough into the muffin tin,
8. Use a spoon to dig a hole in the middle.
9. Place the grated cheese in the holes and sprinkle a teaspoon of the garlic butter mixture on top.
10. Cover the grated cheese with the remaining dough and remaining garlic butter mixture, then sprinkle with Shanghai salt.
11. Place in the oven and Burn for 25 minutes or until golden brown.
12. After removing from the oven, let them cool on the wire rack
13. Enjoy delicious garlic bread muffins and cheese.

Coconut Zucchini Muffins

Ingredients:

- 6 large eggs
-
- 1/5 cup whey protein
-
- 1/8 teaspoon cloves
-
- 1/2 cup tower
-
- 1/5 cup melted butter
-
- 2/4 cup coconut flour
-
- 1/2 cup chopped nuts

  1 teaspoon baking soda

  A tablespoon of water

  2 cups chopped zucchini

  1/2 teaspoon ginger

  1 teaspoon cinnamon

  salt

address:

1. Heat the oven or cookware to 380 ° F, then place the muffin tin in it to prepare the muffin tin.
2. Place the chopped zucchini in the sieve of the sink and sprinkle with a little salt.
3. Drain for 65 minutes, then extract as much liquid as possible from the zucchini.
4. Take a large dish and add baking soda, coconut flour, spices, protein powder, sweetener, and salt.
5. Mix all ingredients.
6. Add water, eggs, butter, and zucchini to the mixture
7. Continue stirring until a thick paste form.
8. Add chopped nuts and pour the batter into the muffin tin in the muffin tin.
9. Place in the preheated oven for 25 minutes, or until the top becomes golden brown.
10. Eradicate from the oven after cooking, fresh, and enjoy delicious coconut and zucchini muffins.

Cinnamon and Apple Spice Muffins

Prepare information:

Ingredients:
- 4 large eggs
- 3/4 cup granulated stevia
- 1 teaspoon vanilla extract
- 1 Teaspoon ground cinnamon
- 1/5 cup unsweetened almond milk
- 2 1/2 cup superfine almond flour

4 ounces Granny Smith apple, peeled, cored, diced

1 teaspoon cereal-free baking powder

1/5 cup butter

1/2 teaspoon sea salt

address:

1. Heat the oven or cookware at a temperature of 380 ° F, then align on the muffin tray to prepare the muffin tray.

.

Put 2 baking powder, almond powder, cinnamon powder, stevia granules and salt into a medium-sized dish.

Mix until all ingredients are thoroughly mixed.

3. Add butter to the mixture and stir until uniform.
4. Put almond milk, vanilla extract and eggs in another dish and mix well.
5. Add egg mixture to almond flour mixture
6. Continue to mix until a smooth dough is formed.
7. Add diced apples to the dough, mix well, then put in the muffin tin in the muffin tin.
8. Put the oven in the oven for 25 minutes,
9. Or until you touch the bread and find the bread grows up.
10. Finally, eradicate from the oven, cold and enjoy delicious muffins.

Cranberry Orange Bread

Ingredients:

- 2 cups chopped fresh blueberries
-
- 9 tablespoons coconut flour
-
- 1 1/3 teaspoon orange juice
-
- 3 tablespoons monk fruit powder
-
- 5 eggs
-
- 1 1/3 teaspoon baking powder
-

  1 yellow

  2 Tablespoon sour cream

  9 tablespoons melted butter

  1 Teaspoon vanilla

  2/4 cup fishing fish meal

  1/5 teaspoon frosting:

- 2 Tablespoon monk fruit powder
-
- 1/2 tablespoon melted butter

  Heavy cream

address:

1. Heat the oven or cookware to 380 ° F and prepare a plain bread tray with parchment paper.
2. Mix melted butter, 2/4 cups of monk fruit, orange juice, egg yolk, vanilla extract, sour cream, and eggs.
3. Mix all ingredients until uniform.
4. Add baking soda, coconut flour and salt to the mixture
5. Stir until the dough is ready.
6. Put chopped blueberries in a dish,
7. And keep stirring until the blueberries are completely covered.
8. Put the coated blueberries in the dough and mix them well, then put the dough in the bread tray.

9. Burn it in the oven for 55 minutes, or insert the knife into the bread until clean.
10. Add a little cream, 2 tablespoons of monk fruit and half tablespoons of melted butter to the dish to prepare the frosting.
11. Spread on hot bread and enjoy.
11.

Lemon and Poppy Seed Roll

Ingredients:

- 3 eggs
-
- 1/5 cup coconut flour
-
- 1/5 teaspoon xanthan gum
-
- 1 Tablespoon of poppy seeds
- 2 Tablespoon sour cream
-
- 1/5 cup almond flour
-
- 1/2 teaspoon vanilla extract
-

1/2 teaspoon baking soda

2 Heavy cream

1/3 cup low-calorie natural sweetener

3 1 tablespoon butter

1 slice lemon

1/2 teaspoon salt

address:

Heat the oven or cookware to 380 ° F and prepare a muffin pan lined with paper muffin pans.

2. Take a dish and add coconut flour, baking powder, poppy seeds, almond flour, lemon peel, xanthan gum, sweetener and salt.
3. Mix all the ingredients until they are even.
4. Break the eggs, put them in a dish and mix them with an electric mixer.
5. Add vanilla extract, butter and sour cream to the mixture and stir until all ingredients are well mixed.

6. Mix flour mixture with egg mixture, then add heavy cream.
7. Continue stirring until a thick paste form.
8. Burn in the oven for 25 minutes, or until you find a good quality tan.
9. Take them out of the oven after cooking and enjoy the incredible poppy seed and lemon muffins.

Blueberry muffins

Ingredients:

- 2 large eggs
-
- 1/5 cup butter
-
- 70g fresh blueberries
-
- 3 Cup of almond flour
-
- 1 teaspoon vanilla extract
- 3 tablespoons almond milk

   25 drops of liquid stevia

   3 teaspoons baking soda

   1/5 cup erythritol

   1/5 teaspoon pink salt

address:

1. Heat the oven or cookware to 380 ° F, then prepare a muffin pan on a paper muffin pan lining.
2. Place the butter in a large dish, then place it in the microwave for 40 seconds or until it melts.
3. Add eggs, almond flour, vanilla extract, almond milk, stevia liquid, baking powder, erythritol and salt to the melted butter.
4. Mix all the ingredients until they are even.
5. Put fresh blueberries into the mixture wisely.
6. Transfer the dough to the muffin tin.
7. Place it in the oven and Burn for 25 minutes, or until the top becomes golden brown.
8. After cooking, Eradicate it from the oven,
9. Let it cool for a few minutes, then try the delicious blueberry-flavored muffins.

Chapter 5

Low-carb chocolate candy

Some of the delicious chocolate and dessert items for young chefs

Chocolate cup and toasted almonds

Ingredients: 3 1/2 ounces butter

4 tablespoons cocoa

1 drop vanilla extract

1 1/2 cups almond flour 4 tablespoons sweetener, slightly salted

You can choose chocolate chips without sugar and nuts

address:

1. Dip butter at room temperature.

2. Mix all ingredients until uniform.

Combine nuts and chocolate chips.

3. Form a ball, wrap it in parchment and place it in the refrigerator for 16 minutes.

4. Preheat the oven to 325ºF.

5. Eradicate the dough from the refrigerator. Make 16 slightly hardened meatballs and Burn them on the baking sheet for about 16 minutes.

6. Turn off the cooler and let it cool in the open oven.

Chocolate bomb

Ingredients: 3 1/2 ounces cheese with milk

2 powdered sugar

3 1/2 ounces chopped chocolate

1 tablespoon Bailey (optional)

address:

1. Melt 2 1/2 ounces, then stir the chocolate in a water bath or microwave until smooth.

2. Brush the sides of 6 cups of chocolate muffins with a brush or fingers, and then put it in the refrigerator for a few minutes.

3. Mix cheese, powdered sugar and liqueur (if applicable) in a dish.

4. Use a spoon to fill the muffin dish with the cheese mixture.

5. Melt the remaining chocolate and place it on the cheese mixture.

6. Freeze the mussels with a pump until settling.

Chocolate and coconut bombs

Ingredients:

1/2 cup salted coconut flakes

1/2 cup coconut oil

3 tablespoons erythritol

1/2 cup coconut oil

2 ounces of dark chocolate (without added sugar, 85% or more cocoa powder)

1. **address:**
2. Melt the coconut oil mixture in the microwave for 50 seconds to 1 minute,
3. Then mix thoroughly.

2. Add coconut flakes and sweetener and mix again.

3. Pour the mixture into an ice tray (or silicone mold) and freeze for 40 minutes.
4. Melt the dark chocolate in the microwave for 1 minute.
5. A tablespoon of coconut chocolate falls on each bomb.

Fried chocolate bomb chain

Ingredients:

3/4-ounce cocoa butter

7 ounces of soft cheese (Macapon or Filadafia)

1-ounce sweetener (erythritol or erythritol and stevia)

3 tablespoons cocoa powder

½ bar chocolate or sugar-free homemade chocolate

1. **address:**

2. Mix cheese, sweetener and cocoa powder until all goes well.
3. If erythritol is slightly soluble, you can grind it in a coffee grinder or pour a small amount of boiling water,
4. Then pour the syrup into the batter
5. Roll the mixture into 16 small balls, put a rope in each small ball,
6. And freeze in the refrigerator for 1 1/2 hours.
4. Melt chocolate and cocoa butter in a water bath and mix thoroughly.
5. Eradicate the grease gun and let the chocolate harden in the refrigerator.

Chocolate high heels with big sunflower seeds chocolate

Ingredients:

3 1/2 ounces sunflower seeds, roasted, chopped

7 Angsey yellow oil melts

3 teaspoons sweetener (e.g. Stevie)

3 tablespoons cocoa powder, vanilla or vanilla extract

address:

1. Mix all dry ingredients.

2. Add melted butter and vanilla and mix well.

3. Pour the mixture into a silicone mold and let it cool.

Coconut chocolate

Ingredients:

Equipped with equipment

. 1-ounce butter or coconut oil, melted

4 ounces almond flour

2 ounces of erythritol

2 eggs

1 1/2 tablespoons cocoa powder (roasted)

1/2 teaspoon vanilla or vanilla extract, the product tastes 9 times as dark chocolate

address:

1. Beat eggs with erythritol.

2. In addition to chocolate, add other ingredients to the egg. Mix gently

3. Divide the dough into 9 parts to form granules. Put a piece of chocolate on each ball. Roll each ball in your hand to completely wrap the chocolate.

6. Burn on a parchment-lined baking sheet at 400 ° F for 25 to 30 minutes.

7. Store it in the refrigerator, and then store it in the refrigerator.

The chocolate will be spread out in advance without any surprises.

Keto Chocolate Cookies Keto Chocolate Ice Cream Shower

Ingredients:

3/4 cup almond flour

1/2 cup coconut oil

1/5 cup almond paste

1 tablespoon maple syrup

1/5 cup unsweetened chocolate, thinly sliced

address

1. Place almond paste and coconut oil in a microwave-safe dish.
2. The mixture is melted by heating.

2. Mix the chocolate with the oil and marzipan mixture.

3. Add maple syrup and almond flour.

4. Spread the mixture on a 1 cm thick tray and put it in the refrigerator for about an hour.

5. Cut the cold mixture into 6 biscuits and place in the refrigerator.

Shower and chocolate ice cream

Ingredients:

2 1/2 ounces coconut cream

2 ounces butter or coconut oil

1 tablespoon jar

1 teaspoon vanilla extract

1 2/4 cup coconut milk

. 1-3 teaspoons liquid sweetener

. 4 yellow eggs

1/8 teaspoon xanthan gum (optional)

address:

1. Beat the yellow eggs.

2. Heat 1/2 cup coconut milk and vanilla extract in a small pot over low heat.

3. Slowly stir the beef and vanilla milk into the egg yolk, then gently stir.

 Operate gradually so that the yolk does not freeze.

 Cook the egg yolk mixture for 5 to 7 minutes with stirring until the mixture thickens.

Don't let it cook. Then let the mixture cool.

4. If using xanthan gum, mix it with liquid sweetener.

5. Slowly pour the cold sweetener into the whipped milk mixture.

 If you do not want to use xanthan gum, you can pour all sweeteners into the milk at the same time.

   8. The coconut then mixes the milk and egg yolk mixture with cocoa butter and coconut cream.

   9. Stir all ingredients for 1 to 2 minutes.

7. You can freeze the mixture with an ice cream machine.

8. Place the ice cubes in the refrigerator for about 3 to 4 hours.

cream.

Ketone and coconut chocolate

Ingredients:

3 ounces melted butter

4 tablespoons coconut flakes

1-ounce solid hash

1 tablespoon cocoa powder

1 teaspoon granulated sweetener

1 teaspoon vanilla extract

1. **address:**

2. Melt butter. Mix all the ingredients and add it to the melted butter.
3. Mix well
4. Use a small rectangular pan. Pour the mixture into it.
5. Place the pan in the refrigerator for 1 to 4 hours.

If it is hard, eradicate it from the refrigerator and cut the hard batter into 40 pieces of caramel.

Coconut ketose

Ingredients:

peanut butter

1-ounce coconut oil, melted

2 1/2 ounces coconut flakes

. 1 to 3 teaspoons sweetener

1 teaspoon vanilla extract

3 teaspoons cocoa

2 oz dark chocolate glaze (optional)

address:

1. Mix all ingredients except dark chocolate in a dish.

2. Sprinkle the mixture on the rectangular surface of the smooth edge of the pot with a spatula. Store in the refrigerator for 40 to 65 minutes.

3. If you use chocolate, melt it in a water bath or microwave.

3. Pour the melted chocolate onto the cold caramel, and then cool until it hardens. Cut the caramel into 14 pieces. Keep it cool.

One piece: 174 calories, 16.8g fat, 3.8g protein, 6.6g carbohydrate.

Dark chocolate ketone pump

16 servings in 16 minutes

Equipped with equipment

1/2-ounce cocoa powder

2 ounces of cocoa butter

1/2-ounce erythritol powder

8 drops of stevia 1 teaspoon vanilla nut extract, you can taste dried fruits and decorate with sesame

- **address:**
- Melt cocoa butter in a low-calorie water bath. The most important thing is not to cook!
- After melting, put in a blender and add cocoa powder, erythritol, stevia and vanilla.
- Mix until everything goes well.
- Pour the mixture into the tenth silicone mold.

- Garnish with nuts, berries and sesame seeds.
- Place the mussels in the refrigerator for 16 minutes and then put them in the refrigerator.
- Each (excluding side dishes): 50 calories, 0.3 g protein, 5.2 g fat, carbohydrate composition
- The total sugar is 0.9 grams and 0.1 grams.

Lightweight chocolate and coconut high heels

Ingredients:

2 cups salted macadamia

2 to 4 tablespoons of coconut oil (melted, used in most solid fat pumps)

1 teaspoon vanilla extract (optional)

1/3 cup sweetener powder

1/5 cup of cocoa powder

address:

1. Place macadamia nuts in a food processor or sturdy blender and extract them into small pieces.

2. Add melted coconut oil to the nuts and add vanilla if necessary.

Mash until it forms a shell.

3. Pour cocoa powder and sweetener gradually into the batter while stirring.

4. Mix ingredients gently.

4. Parchment fanatics in the cake jar.

Place the dough evenly in the mold.

5. Freeze for about 40 minutes to harden.

Berry fat gun

Ingredients:

2 cups of fruit at the waist

2 cup dates

2 cups blackberries

2 cocoa powder

1/5 teaspoon nutmeg

No need to decorate the mounting shaft

address:

1. Tare date.

2. Wash the cashews and blackberries thoroughly.

Dry towels.

3. Mix all the ingredients in the food processor. Pour the mixture into the mold (for pancakes). Place the mixture in the refrigerator for 1 hour.

Blueberry Ketone Butter Gun

Ingredients:

7 ounces blueberries (frozen)

7 Angus butter, soft technology

3 ounces coconut oil

4 5 1/2 ounces almond flour granules erythritol flavor

2 tablespoons lemon juice

1. **address:**

2. Cook blueberries over medium heat in a coated pan.
3. Cook the blueberries in enough boiling water for 16 to 16 minutes, or until most of the liquid has evaporated. Don't forget to move

2. Crush the blueberries with flour and erythritol in a food processor.

3. Mix all remaining ingredients to get a smooth purple dough.

4. Freeze the mixture for 16 minutes.

5. Eradicate the dough from the refrigerator.

6. Shape the mixture into 8 balls.

Roll the ball into the erythritol granules to get the final appearance.

7. Cool the ball in the refrigerator for at least 1 hour.

Strawberry cream

Ingredients:

Equipped with equipment

2 cups fresh or frozen strawberries

4 tablespoons unsalted yellow oil

2 tablespoons stevia or erythritol

Temperature chamber. 8 ounces of dry cream cheese

4 tablespoons unsalted yellow oil

A few drops of vanilla extract (optional)

address:

1. Stir the strawberries and vanilla in a small blender until chopped.

2. Melt cream cheese and butter in two dishes. mixing.

3. Use a fork to push the strawberries into a medium-sized dish.

Add cream cheese mixture.

4. Homogenize the mixture in a muffin pan on the ground, then place in the refrigerator for at least 40 minutes.

Pudding lemon and blackberry

Ingredients:

¼ cup coconut flour

5 large eggs

2 tablespoons balsam

2 tablespoons coconut oil

2 tablespoons milk

2 tablespoons lemon erythritol

3 teaspoons lemon juice

1/2 cup black fruit

16 drops of margarita

address:

1. Preheat the oven to 350ºF.

2. Separate yellow and white eggs.

Beat egg yolks to light yellow.

Add erythritol and stevia and mix well.

3. Add fat cream, coconut oil and lemon juice.

4. Wash and grind the lemon. Add dish to mixture and stir.

5. Add coconut flour and baking powder.

6. Mix all ingredients.

7. Add the blackberries to the mixture.

8. Squeeze the berries gently.

9. Burn the pudding for 25 to 30 minutes.

Lemon Cheese Pancakes Fried Lemon Coconut Mussels

Ingredients:

Equipped with equipment

½ pound dry cream cheese

2 ounces of fat cream

1 tablespoon lemon juice

1 teaspoon liquid stevia1 teaspoon lemon zest and vanilla

address:

1. Put cream cheese and cream in a dish.
2. Mix them with a blender until a uniform paste is obtained.
3. Add stevia, lemon juice, vanilla and lemon zest.
4. Mix well
4. Place the mixture in the pan and consume immediately.
5. Let it harden in the refrigerator for two hours for best results.

Coconut and lemon bomb

Ingredients:

2 cups coconut oil

1 chopped lemon slice

1 tablespoon coconut cream

1 teaspoon vanilla extract

3 tablespoons lemon juice

1 tablespoon erythritol or xylitol

A little salt

address:

1. Place all ingredients in a blender and mix thoroughly.

2. Wrap the mixture in parchment paper and place in the refrigerator for 40 minutes.

3. Eradicate the mixture from the refrigerator, smooth it and roll into 16 balls.

Freeze again in the refrigerator for 40 minutes.

Coconut cake, poppy seeds and lemon

Ingredients:

2 ounces coconut flour

4 large eggs

½ cup unsweetened yogurt

2 ounces coconut oil

2 tablespoons coconut flakes

3 teaspoons baking powder 1 teaspoon vanilla powder

1 lemon

2 tablespoons poppy seeds

address:

1. Preheat the oven to 350ºF.

2. Crush the eggs.

Add coconut flour, melted coconut oil, yogurt, baking powder and vanilla.

Stir all ingredients until smooth.

Let the dough rest for five minutes.

3. Wash the peeled lemons.
4. Then cut off the top layer of the skin
5. Cut into a blender
6. Squeeze lemon juice,
7. Add the juice, peel it into a mixture and mix.
6. With movable side edge shape.
7. Lubricate with parchment and coconut oil.
8. Place the dough on paper.
9. Decorate the top of the cake with coconut flakes and poppy seeds.
10. Burn for 25 to 40 minutes.

Lemon Pump Ketone

Ingredients:

1 1/5-ounce cream

2 1/2 ounces butter

5 teaspoons lemon juice

7 1/2 ounces of dry cream cheese

address:

1. Melted butter.

2. Insert the cheese puree with a fork.

3. Mix all ingredients into 6 balls.

4. Place in the refrigerator for 1 hour.

Nut and berry pancakes

Ingredients:

4 ounces unsweetened peanut butter

1-ounce cocoa powder

1 large egg

1/5 teaspoon soda

1/5 teaspoon marinated vinegar and nuts,

Almonds, hazelnuts and walnuts (2 oz each)

Dried or fresh berries (cranberry or cranberry)

Boil it down

address:

1. Preheat the oven to 350ºF.
2. Put peanut butter and cocoa powder in a deep dish.

Add eggs to beat.

Add soda, vinegar and salt.

Mix the ingredients with a blender to get a smooth creamy paste.

3. Add nuts or berries in moderation.

4. Fill the water tank with eggs and oven cake. Burn for 16 to 25 minutes.

Raspberry and lemon ice pump

Ingredients:

1/5 cup coconut oil

2 cups coconut milk

1/5 cup yogurt

1/5 cup butter 3 1/2 ounces raspberry juice 1/2 lemon

25 drops of liquid stevia

address:

1. Mix all ingredients in a blender until the raspberries are mixed with the rest of the product.

2. Filter the mixture to Eradicate raspberry seeds.

This is important because full ice pump seeds can irritate the tongue.

2. Decant the mixture.

5. Silicone mold, freeze for 2 hours.

Strawberry Ketone Fat Pump

Ingredients:

1/5 cup coconut flakes

3/4 cup almond flour

3/4 cup coconut flour

4 medium berries

1 teaspoon vanilla extract

1 to 2 tablespoons coconut oil

1 tablespoon sweet chrysanthemum

address:

1. In high-speed food processors
2. Obtain all ingredients except coconut leaves until the mixture is homogeneous.

2. Divide the mixture into 25 portions and roll each piece into a ball.
3. Roll the ball wisely onto the coconut flakes.
4. Store in the refrigerator for 1 hour.

Strawberries are used to soften fat pumps
And prevent excessive carbohydrates.

Carrot pancakes

Ingredients:

2 ounces almond flour

1-ounce coconut flour

2 tablespoons baking soda

2 hard Angsi fruits

1 teaspoon chia seeds

4 carrots, chopped Angsi Bu

4 large eggs

4 Philadelphia Angsi dry cream cheese

4 ounces of yogurt (40%)

. 3 ounces yellow vanilla oil

Mistletoe

salt

address:

1. Preheat the oven to 325ºF.

2. Prepare cream.

Put cream cheese, sour cream and herbs in a blender.

Mix well until everything is normal.

Let the mixture sit down.

3. Mix coconut and almond flour, chia seeds and nuts.
4. Add baking powder, salt and cinnamon powder.
5. Grind all these dry ingredients in the flour. You may encounter a big problem.

4. Chopped carrots.

5. Separate the yellow eggs from the eggs.

Beat egg whites to increase air.

Mix egg yolks.

6. Melt the butter and put it in the refrigerator.

Mix white with egg yolk.

Add melted butter. Mix again.

7. Add the dry ingredients to the mixture: mix flour, nuts and seeds.

Mix gently by hand or blender.

8. Place the carrots evenly under the dough.

9. Place the dough on the baking sheet and burn for 50 minutes.

16. Let the pancakes cool and cut into thin slices.

Apply each layer of cream. Put the cake in the refrigerator overnight.

Another low-carb food

Almond Cookies

Ingredients:

2 cups almond flour

1/2 cup erythritol

1/5 cup yellow oil

2 eggs

1 teaspoon vanilla extract 1 teaspoon almonds

address:

1. Preheat the oven to 405ºF.
2. While heating in the oven, mix almond flour, erythritol, cinnamon powder and a small amount of salt in a dish.
3. Beat eggs in a small dish.

Add butter and vanilla.

Eradicate

4. Mix the dry ingredients with the egg mixture until uniform.

5. Cut the dough into small circles with a spoon.

6. Decorate the circle with half almonds.

7. Spread the butter paper on the baking tray. Place the dry cake on top.

8. Burn for 16 to 20 minutes.

Coconut fat pump Keto coconut oil pump

Ingredients:

Equipped with equipment

2 ounces melted coconut oil

1 1/2-ounce child

6 1/2 ounces of mascarpone or cream cheese, softened at room temperature

3 teaspoons of coconut leaves and 2 tablespoons of tablespoons

1 teaspoon sweetener or seasoning

1/2-ounce cocoa butter (optional)

address:

1. If using coconut oil and cocoa butter, melt it in a water bath or microwave.

2. Add all other ingredients to the oil to make the mixture even,

Then put in the refrigerator for 16 minutes.

If cocoa butter is not used, it should be refrigerated for 25 minutes.

3. Roll 16 walnut balls and cool the mixture.

4. Roll them into coconut flakes.

5. Store in the refrigerator for 25-40 minutes.

You can drink tea or coffee according to your taste. These sweet coconut fat pumps with pine nuts and coconut flakes have a creamy taste.

Coconut ketone oil pump

Ingredients:

4 dried Angsi cream cheese

1/2 cup milk oil

1 teaspoon vanilla orange

1/2 cup coconut oil

16 drops of margarita

address:

1. Mix all ingredients in a blender.
2. If the ingredients are difficult to mix, straighten them in the microwave.
2. Freeze the mixture in a silicone mold for 3 to 4 hours.
3. After freezing, Eradicate the pump from the mold and store it in the refrigerator.

Cheese balls

Ingredients:

1-pound cheese (18% fat content)

11 ounces butter (can use coconut butter)

2 1/2 ounces dark chocolate

1 2/4 ounce cream (40-45%)

address:

1. Combine cheese and sucrose.

2. Add 7 ounces of soft butter or melted coconut oil to the mixture.

3. Mix all ingredients evenly until all ingredients are mixed together.

Mix 11 balls. Freeze for 16 to 25 minutes.

4. Melt chocolate and 4 ounces of butter in a pan or water bath.

5. Cook for 5 to 7 minutes, then gradually add the cream.

 Shake the mixture.

6. Eradicate the cheese balls from the refrigerator and pour chocolate glaze on them.

7. When the time is up, freeze the pump for 25 minutes.

 However, it is best to freeze them for 65 to 90 minutes.

Greer Ferrero-Rocher-Qin Kai

"Truffle" Ketone

Ingredients:

½ cup coffee and double espresso

1/5 cup melted yellow oil

1/5 cup of milk

1/5 cup of sweetener of your choice

1/2 cup yellow oil

1 tablespoon of milk (optional)

1 teaspoon vanilla extract

A little salt

1. **address:**
2. Place all ingredients in the food processor.
3. Beat at high speed until launch.
4. Pour into the mold
5. And store in the refrigerator for 40 minutes.

Greer Ferrero-Rocher-Qin Kai

16 servings in 1 hour and 16 minutes

Equipped with equipment

3 1/2 ounces hazelnut powder 2 ounces coconut oil erythritol powder

3 1/2 ounces unsweetened chocolate

1 teaspoon unsweetened vanilla extract ½ tablespoon cocoa powder

Chopped hazelnuts and 16 whole hazelnuts Ge Kind

address:

1. Melt sugar-free chocolate in a water bath.

2. If necessary, melt coconut oil in the microwave.

3. Put chopped hazelnuts, erythritol powder, melted coconut oil, cocoa powder and vanilla extract in a food processor
And mix at high speed for about 40 to 50 seconds.

4. Add the melted chocolate and mix for another 16 seconds.

5. Let the mixture cool in the refrigerator and shape 16 balls by hand.

6. Place the whole hazelnut in the middle of each grease gun, and then use the chopped hazelnut to roll the ball. cold

"Truffle" Ketone

Ingredients:

3 1/2 ounces yellow oil

2 ounces of cocoa powder

11 ounces of cream cheese

1 to 3 tablespoons erythritol (or seasoning)

1 tablespoon freshly ground black coffee

1 teaspoon instant coffee powder

A few drops of vanilla extract

address:

1. Cream cheese is mixed with cocoa powder, coffee, instant coffee powder and hemi erythritol.

2. Add vanilla extract and soft butter to the mixture.

 Stir until smooth.

   3. A chocolate mixture forming 6 balls.

   4. Roll them into the rest of the cocoa powder.

   5. Place it on paper and let it cool.

3. Please Eradicate from the refrigerator for a few minutes before serving.

Philadelphia Cream Cheese Ketone Pump

Ingredients:

5 1/2-ounce Philadelphia cream cheese

butter

2 ounces 1/2 teaspoon coconut oil, erythritol, stevia granules or liquid sweetener, vanilla extract or vanilla extract

Ketone chocolate topping ingredients:

1-ounce cocoa powder

1 tablespoon coconut oil or stevia extract with cocoa butter

address:

1. Stir and pump all ingredients through the food processor until uniform.

2. Gradually add erythritol, occasionally slightly sweet.

You will need about half a teaspoon of erythritol and a drop of sativoside.

Stir until everything is completely dissolved.

3. Use a small mold or silicone muffin to transfer the mixture to the mold and fill 3/4.

4. Place the pump in the refrigerator for 16 to 25 minutes.

5. At the same time, prepare the keto chocolate filling.

Heat chopped cocoa with coconut oil in a water bath. Just add stevia extract to get more sweetness! Eradicate

When the mixture is completely mixed, eradicate it from the fire and allow it to cool slightly.

6. Eradicate the ketone pump from the freezer and pour the chocolate mixture on it.

7. Store in the refrigerator for another 2 hours.

Bite from Ketone Brownie

Ingredients:

almond flour

soft butter

1 teaspoon erythritol powder

1 1/2 ounces cocoa powder for frying

1 teaspoon vanilla extract, sugar-free

address:

1. Mix all the ingredients in the dish with a spoon.

2. Do 8 balls. If the oil in the grease gun is too soft to roll, place the mixture in the refrigerator

for about 16 minutes. Allow the ball to cool after 16 to 16 minutes.

Easter "pancakes"

Ingredients:

9 ounces cream cheese (mascarpone)

Temperature chamber. 7 ounces butter 1 teaspoon sweetener (granular stevia), slightly scented herbs

2 ounces of whole sweet-sour cream and 1 teaspoon of sweetener (e.g. stevia)

manual

1. Add sweetener, vanilla extract and blueberries, mix cream cheese and butter.

2. Completely fill the mold (for large pancakes) for at least two hours and then cool.
3. Flip the mold, and then Eradicate the "pancake" wisely.
4. Serve with sweet and sour cream.

Ketone Fund Award

Ingredients:

3 1/2 ounces yellow oil

1/2 cup coconut cream

2 cups coconut flakes

1 teaspoon sweetener

1 teaspoon vanilla extract

3-4 tablespoons coconut oil

½ semi-sweet sugar-free chocolate (or homemade chocolate)

1. **address:**
2. Mix flakes, cream, sweetener, vanilla and coconut oil in a dish.
3. Then shape 16 balls by hand. Freeze for 2 hours.

2. Melt chocolate and butter in a water bath or microwave.

Pour chocolate wisely into the pump, then put it back in the refrigerator until it is full.

Keto Raffaella 16 pieces per hour

Ingredients:

almond oil

3 1/2 ounces coconut cream

3/4-ounce coconut oil (optional)

Erythritol odor gas

1 teaspoon vanilla extract

4 Macsamia or apricot Angsi seeds

1 1/2 ounces chopped coconut

address:

1. In a small dish, grind almond butter and coconut cream until smooth.

2. Add sweetener and vanilla extract (add coconut oil if necessary).

Place the mixture of almond and coconut cream in the refrigerator for about 25 minutes.

4. Eradicate coconut and almond cream from the refrigerator.

5. The consistency should be sufficient to form 16 balls. If the almond and coconut cream is too thin, return it to the refrigerator for 16 to 25 minutes.

3. Slide the nut onto each ball.

4. Put the chopped coconut into the dish.

Roll almond and coconut balls into grated coconut.

Low-carb egg cheese cake

Ingredients:

1/3 cup melted yellow oil

2 cups almond flour

3 tablespoons erythritol, chopped

1/5 cup erythritol powder

3 large eggs

1 teaspoon vanilla extract

2 pounds cream cheese (softened)

1 tablespoon lemon juice

address:

1. Preheat the oven to 400ºF. Grease a 9-inch spring pan or wrap parchment paper on the floor.
2. In a medium dish, mix almond flour, melted butter, erythritol and vanilla extract.
 The dough will crack.
3. Place the dough in a tin can and make it smooth.
 burn for 16 to 12 minutes until golden brown.
4. Cool for 16 minutes.
5. Simultaneously mix cream cheese and powdered sweetener.
Beat the eggs with a blender. Add lemon juice and vanilla extract to the beaten eggs.
(The mixer remains in a low or medium state).
   6. Pour the filling into the pancake mold. Cook for 50 to 55 minutes.
   7. If you Eradicate the cheesecake from the oven, it may stick to the sides of the pan.
   8. Don't worry about moving the knife over the edge (do not open the spring). Let the

cake cool to room temperature. Do not try to Eradicate the cake from the mold before cooling.

Naples grease gun

Ingredients:

1/2 cup sour cream

1/2 cup butter chili barrier

2 tablespoons erythritol

25 drops of margarita

2 medium-sized strawberry fruits

1/2 cup yellow oil

1/2 cup coconut oil

2 tablespoons cocoa powder 1 teaspoon vanilla extract

address:

1. Mix all ingredients except cocoa powder, vanilla and strawberry in a blender.

2. Homogenize the mixture in three dishes. Put cocoa powder in one dish, vanilla in another dish, and strawberries in a third dish. Mix each dish.

3. Fill the silicone mold or the top of the lubricated 1/3 muffin with chocolate mixture.

 Place in the refrigerator for 40 minutes.

   6. After 40 minutes, Eradicate the pot and pour the vanilla mixture into the lower third.

   7. Freeze for 40 minutes.

5. Add the strawberry mixture after freezing.

6. Freeze the pump for one hour.

Keto nuts and peanut butter sweet fruit

Ingredients:

½ cup coconut oil

1 tablespoon cocoa powder

½ teaspoon sweetener ½ teaspoon vanilla, almond, nut, peanut and peanut butter and flavored products with yellow hazelnut oil

address:

1. Prepare a water bath. Melt coconut oil, but don't overheat it.

2. Add cocoa and sweetener to the melted oil. Add vanilla to taste.

You can change the number of ingredients as needed.

Pour half of the contents into the mold.

3. Add peanut butter or peanut butter to each caramel.

Decorate with the rest of the coconut oil mixture, then immediately sprinkle the cocoa powder on the nut food.

Place in the refrigerator to harden.

5. Wait for the syrup to cool before adding sugar.
6. Mix 165 grams of pasta and 40 grams of oil (or your choice).
7. Add a thick layer of chocolate.
8. Then cover the second part of the mixture.
   6. Put candy in the refrigerator. The nuances of ketones.

Pumpkin Pump

Ingredients:

1/3 cup coconut sauce

2 tablespoons coconut oil

2 tablespoons maple syrup

1/2 cup pumpkin head

2 tablespoons pumpkin pie flavor

1 teaspoon vanilla protein powder

2 tablespoons gelatin

address:

1. Melt coconut oil and put in microwave.

2. Mix all the ingredients in the food processor. Press until a smooth mixture form.

3. Pour the mixture into 16 small silicone muffin dishes.

4. Place them in the refrigerator for at least one hour.

Pumpkin Cheese Egg Mousse

- **Ingredients:**
- Lb. cream cheese
  - Pound of unsweetened pumpkin puree
- ½ cup erythritol
  - Teaspoon pure vanilla extract
  - Tablespoon pumpkin pie flavor
- ¾ cup of milk oil

- **address:**
- Mix hand cream cheese and pumpkin in a large dish.
- The mixture should be creamy, smooth and smooth.
- Add vanilla, spices, erythritol and cream to the pumpkin mixture.

- Completely mixed
- 3. Cool the foam before eating.

Made in the USA
Coppell, TX
02 June 2020

26827880R00087